WORLD'S TALLEST BUILDINGS

DANIEL BLYTHE

Badger Publishing Limited
Oldmedow Road,
Hardwick Industrial Estate,
King's Lynn PE30 4JJ
Telephone: 01438 791037
www.badgerlearning.co.uk

4 6 8 10 9 7 5 3

The World's Tallest Buildings ISBN 978-1-78464-119-1

Text © Daniel Blythe 2015

Complete work © Badger Publishing Limited 2015

All rights reserved. No part of this publication may be reproduced, stored in any form or by any means mechanical, electronic, recording or otherwise without the prior permission of the publisher.

The right of Daniel Blythe to be identified as author of this work has been asserted by him in accordance with the Copyright, Designs and Patents Act 1988.

Publisher: Susan Ross
Senior Editor: Danny Pearson
Publishing Assistant: Claire Morgan
Designer: Fiona Grant
Series Consultant: Dee Reid

Photos: Cover Image: VIEW Pictures Ltd / Alamy
Page 5: © Sergey Borisov/Alamy
Page 7: © Kjersti Joergensen/Alamy
Page 8: © Roland Nagy/Alamy
Page 9: © LOOK Die Bildagentur der Fotografen GmbH/Alamy
Page 10: © Steve Vidler/Alamy
Page 11: © Boaz Rottem/Alamy
Page 12: © David Parker/Alamy
Page 13: Image Broker/REX
Page 14: www.som.com
Page 15: © Batchelder/Alamy
Page 16: Paul Brown/REX
Page 17: © Radius Images/Alamy
Page 18: © epa european pressphoto agency b.v./Alamy
Page 19: Imaginechina/REX
Page 20: Cultura/REX
Page 21: Sipa Press/REX
Page 22: © Iain Masterton/Alamy
Page 23: © LatitudeStock/Alamy
Page 24: Ikon Images/REX
Page 25: © I. Glory/Alamy
Page 26: © dpa picture alliance/Alamy
Page 27: © topdog images/Alamy
Page 28: © Andrew Paterson/Alamy

Attempts to contact all copyright holders have been made.
If any omitted would care to contact Badger Learning, we will be happy to make appropriate arrangements.

WORLD'S TALLEST BUILDINGS

Contents

1.	Reach for the skies	5
2.	Jewels of the East	8
3.	Giants of the world	16
4.	Building for the future	24
	Questions	31
	Index	32

Vocabulary

construction	skyscraper
double-decker	squeegee
overtaken	surrounded
reflecting	temperatures

1. REACH FOR THE SKIES

Buildings are getting taller. As cities run out of space, it makes sense to build upwards.

Very tall buildings are often called **skyscrapers**.

If a building is more than 300 metres high it is known as **supertall**, and if it is more than 600 metres high it is known as **megatall**.

Record breakers

In 1930, the world's tallest building was the Woolworth Building in New York. It was 241 metres high.

Then, between 1930 and 1931 it was overtaken by three buildings:

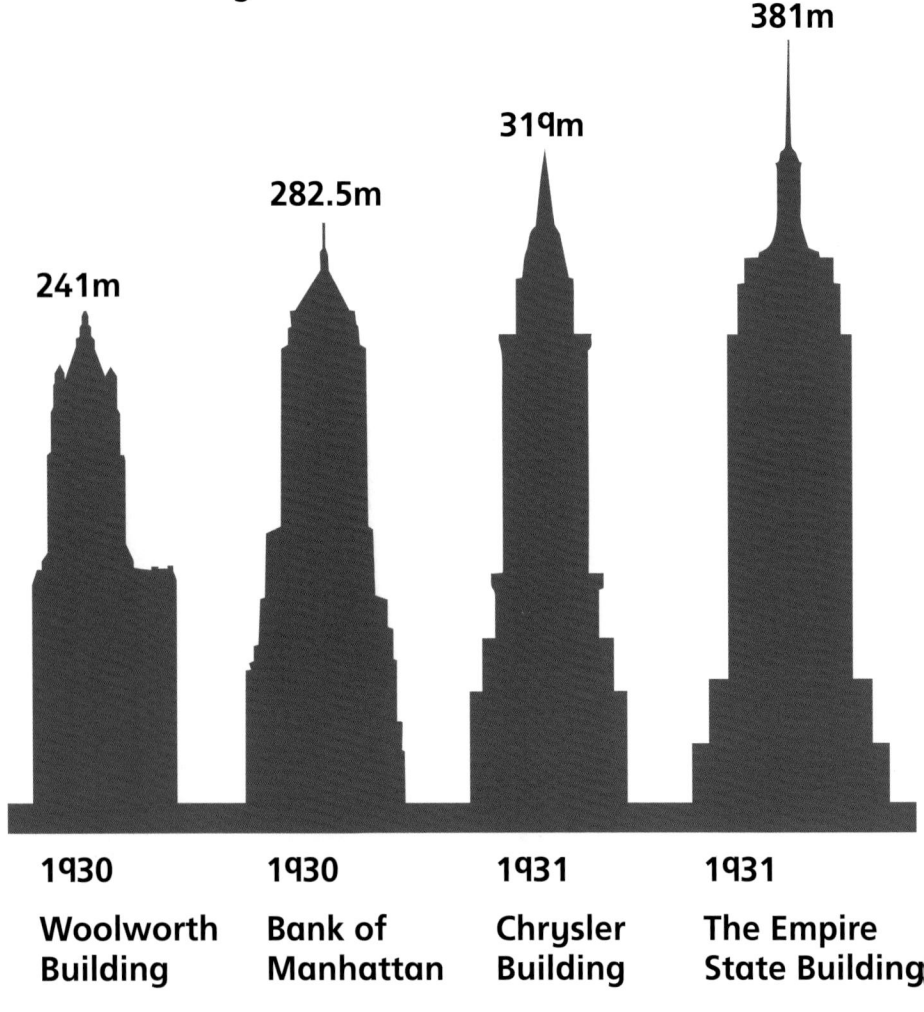

1930	1930	1931	1931
Woolworth Building	Bank of Manhattan	Chrysler Building	The Empire State Building

Today, the world's tallest building is the **Burj Khalifa** in Dubai.

It is 828 metres high. To picture something that tall, think of more than 100 normal houses on top of one another!

It took five years to build.

WOW! facts

You can watch the sun set from the bottom of the Burj Khalifa. Then if you speed up the lift to floor 162 you can watch the sun set again!

2. JEWELS OF THE EAST

The Twin Towers of the East

The Petronas Towers in Malaysia are the ninth and tenth highest buildings in the world today. They are 452 metres tall.

Work began in 1990. To speed up construction, one company was paid to build one tower and another company was paid to build the second tower.

It was a race! Tower two was finished first (but only by a few hours!)

A bridge in the sky

The Petronas Towers are famous for their skybridge where you can cross between the towers.

The skybridge is about halfway up, linking the towers at the 41st and 42nd floors.

Tourists can visit, but queues often start at six o'clock in the morning!

WOW! facts

The Petronas Towers have 32,000 windows!

The International Commerce Centre (called the ICC Tower) is in Hong Kong.

Most of the tower is used for business but there is a hotel with a pool at the very top.

The ICC Tower is 118 storeys high – we think!

Some numbers, such as 4, 14 and 24, are thought to bring bad luck in East Asia and so are often missed off when counting the floors of buildings.

At 484 metres from ground level, this is the eighth highest building in the world.

The ICC Tower would have been taller – but local rules meant that buildings could not be higher than the nearby mountains.

The World Financial Centre in Shanghai at 492 metres is the world's seventh tallest building.

The World Financial Centre took 14 years to build and has an odd shape. Some say it looks like a knife or a bottle opener!

WOW! facts
The open-air platform at floor 91 is the highest open-air deck in the world.

Taipei 101 in Taiwan at 509 metres is the sixth tallest building in the world.

Taipei 101 is said to look like a giant bamboo stalk made out of bluey-green glass.

At the top it has a wind damper, to stop it from shaking in high winds and earthquakes.

Taipei 101 has double-decker lifts! There are 61 lifts in the building and they go up and down at more than 16 metres per second!

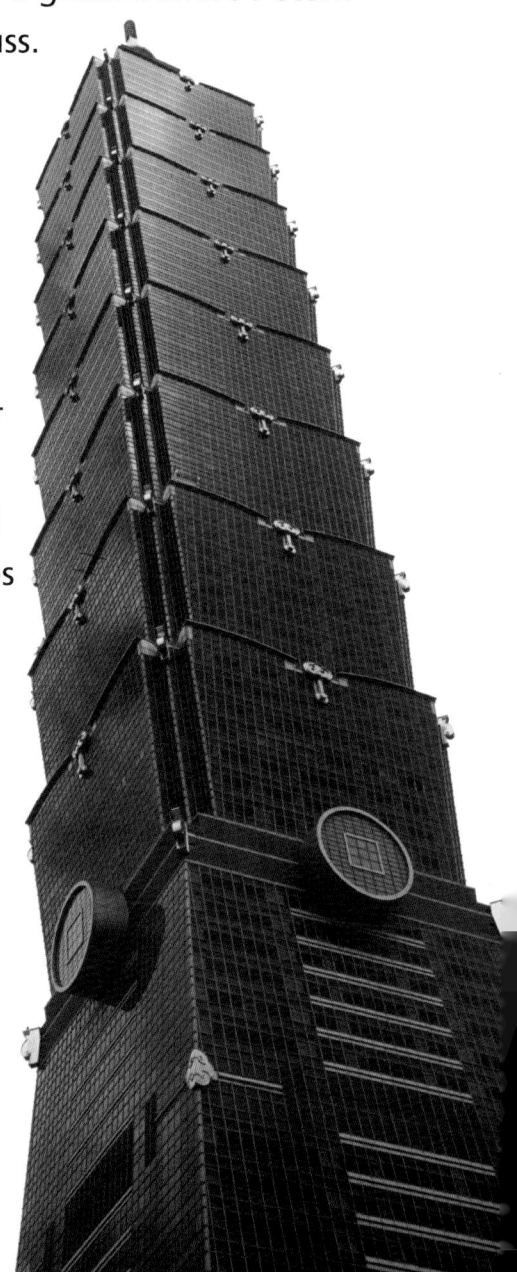

Another building in the top ten tallest buildings is the CTF Finance Centre in Guangzhou, China.

This will be 530 metres when it is finished in 2016 and so it will be the fifth highest building.

It will have one of the world's fastest lifts, taking just 43 seconds to go from the first floor to the 95th floor.

It is also the fastest growing skyscraper in history.

New types of skyscraper

Maybe skyscrapers of the future will not just look like huge glass boxes.

Some architects want skyscrapers to be eco-friendly.

Perhaps skyscrapers of the future could look like fields, farms and woodland in the sky!

WOW! facts

Sixteen of the tallest buildings in the world are in Asia. Europe's tallest building, The Shard in London, doesn't even make the top 70!

3. GIANTS OF THE WORLD

One World Trade Center in New York is the fourth tallest building in the world at 541 metres. It has 104 storeys.

It's the tallest building in the West and replaces the famous Twin Towers of the World Trade Center complex, which were blown up in the attacks of September 11th, 2001.

One World Trade Center was 'topped-out' in 2012.

'Topping-out' is when the last beam or girder at the top of the tower is put in place and the building counts as finished.

Often this is made into a big event and the media are invited.

WOW! facts

One World Trade Center is a bit of a cheat. The top 124 metres are a metal spire.

The top three

The third highest building in the world is the Royal Clock Tower in Mecca, Saudi Arabia – the 'Big Ben of the Muslim world'.

It is 601 metres high and has the biggest clock face in the world. Millions of Muslims set their watches by it.

The minaret and its base have huge speakers to broadcast prayer calls across Mecca.

The second highest building in the world is the Shanghai Tower in China, which is 632 metres tall.

Its design means the wind has limited impact, reducing the materials needed to build it.

The world's tallest building, the Burj Khalifa in Dubai, contains homes and hotels, and is surrounded by parks and a lake.

When it was being built there were as many as 12,000 workers on site!

But how long will it remain the tallest? Other countries want to say that they have the tallest building in the world.

Dicing with death

Some people see tall buildings as a challenge and try to climb them – sometimes legally, and sometimes not!

This is called 'urban climbing', and can be very dangerous.

In the 1980s, Dan Goodwin managed to climb many of the world's highest towers, including the World Trade Center in New York and the Sears Tower in Chicago.

French climber Alain Robert was the first person to climb the Burj Khalifa.

Imagine having to clean 26,000 panes of glass!

That's how many windows there are in Burj Khalifa.

The windows are cleaned by hand! Teams of workers using squeegee mops hang from harnesses and lower themselves down floor by floor.

It takes three months to clean all the windows.

Dangerous buildings

Sometimes there are problems with very tall buildings.

In 2013, the glass in one of London's tallest towers, nicknamed The Walkie Talkie, was found to be reflecting the sun's rays, creating hot spots of up to 107 degrees Celcius (107°C).

This was melting cars on the other side of the street! It has now had a sunshade added to stop this.

WOW! facts
Temperatures of 107°C are hot enough to fry an egg!

4. BUILDING FOR THE FUTURE

So, will buildings ever stop getting taller and taller?

Some experts think so. For one thing, there could be a limit on how high lifts can safely go.

We also have to think about comfort – how high up do we really want to live and work?

Some people are afraid of heights and do not want to be 500 metres up in the air, even in an office!

Another problem is running out of money and materials.

Some planners are talking about the world's first mile-high skyscraper being built this century – but who has the money to pay for it?

Tall towers often take longer to build than expected.

This is sometimes because the money runs out or because the builders find problems which hadn't been thought about. And it's too dangerous to have mistakes in a building over a mile high.

A tiny mistake in the construction could mean that the building tilts dangerously or it could shake in high winds.

One way to make sure the mile-high buildings are stable would be for the skyscrapers to have a wide base like the Eiffel Tower in Paris. Some experts think this could be the way forward.

Perhaps in the future buildings could be higher than the highest mountain. This would mean a building of more than 8848 metres – the height of the world's tallest mountain, Mount Everest!

So, maybe giant skyscrapers like those in sci-fi films could become a reality. If the human race is going to find enough space for everyone to live in the future, we will certainly have to think about it.

WOW! facts

The UK's tallest building outside London is the 47-storey Beetham Tower in Manchester. The giant 'glass blade' on its roof makes a spooky hum, which sounds like a UFO landing!

World's top ten tallest buildings

Number	Building	Year finished	Height in metres	Height in London buses (to nearest bus)
9/10	Petronas Towers, Malaysia	1996	452m	103
8	International Commerce Centre, Hong Kong	2010	484m	110
7	World Financial Centre, Shanghai	2008	492m	112
6	Taipei 101, Taiwan	2004	509m	116
5	CTF Finance Centre, China	2016	530m	121
4	One World Trade Center, USA	2014	541m	124
3	Royal Clock Tower, Mecca, Saudi Arabia	2012	601m	137
2	Shanghai Tower, China	2015	632m	144
1	Burj Khalifa, Dubai	2010	828m	189

WOW! facts

If China's Sky City is finished to plan and on time, it will be 838 metres high, and will overtake both the Shanghai Tower and the Burj Khalifa. It will be as high as 191 London buses!

Questions

Why have buildings been getting higher over the past 100 years? *(page 5)*

What are *supertall* and *megatall* buildings? *(page 5)*

Which part of the world has most of the world's tallest buildings? *(page 15)*

What is the tallest building in Europe? *(page 15)*

Why was The Walkie Talkie dangerous? *(page 23)*

Would you like to live 100 floors up? What would be the best and worst things about living in a skyscraper?

INDEX

Beetham Tower 28
Burj Khalifa 7, 20, 21, 22, 29, 30
Chrysler Building 6
CTF Finance Centre 14, 29
International Commerce Centre 10, 29
One World Trade Center 16-17, 29
Petronas Towers 8-9, 29
Royal Clock Tower 18, 29
Shanghai Tower 19, 29, 30
Sky City 30
skyscraper 5, 14, 15, 25, 27, 28, 31
Taipei 101 13, 29
The Shard 15
The Walkie Talkie 23
Twin Towers 16
urban climbing 21
Woolworth Building 6
World Financial Centre 12, 29